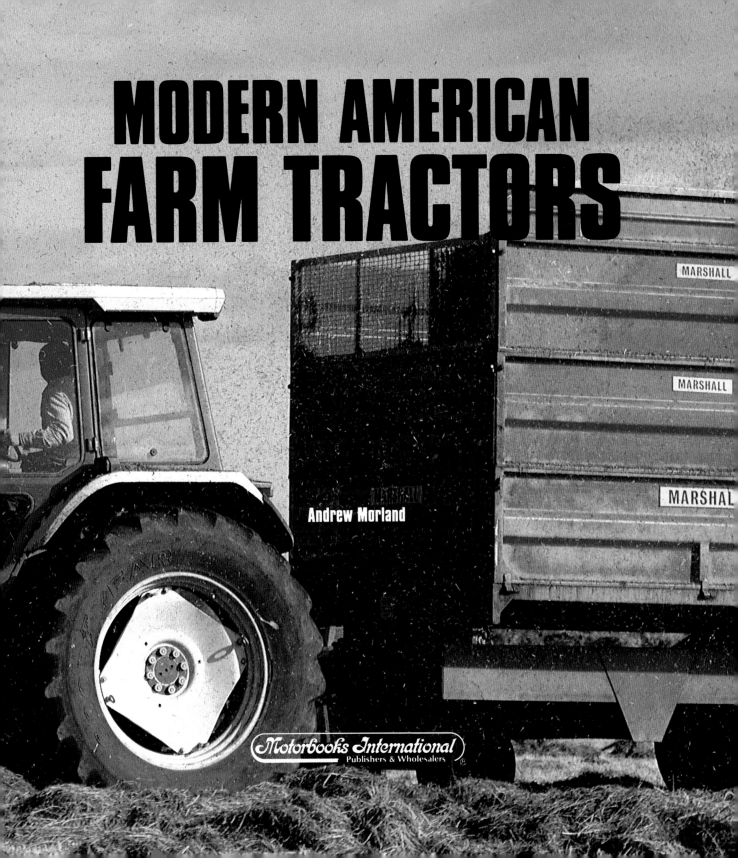

MODERN AMERICAN
FARM TRACTORS

Andrew Morland

MARSHALL

MARSHALL

MARSHAL

Motorbooks International
Publishers & Wholesalers

First published in 1994 by Motorbooks International Publishers & Wholesalers, PO Box 2, 729 Prospect Avenue, Osceola, WI 54020 USA

Motorbooks International is a certified trademark, registered with the United States Patent Office

The information in this book is true and complete to the best of our knowledge. All recommendations are made without any guarantee on the part of the author or Publisher, who also disclaim any liability incurred in connection with the use of this data or specific details

We recognize that some words, model names and designations, for example, mentioned herein are the property of the trademark holder. We use them for identification purposes only. This is not an official publication

Motorbooks International books are also available at discounts in bulk quantity for industrial or sales-promotional use. For details write to Special Sales Manager at the Publisher's address

Library of Congress Cataloging-in-Publication Data

Morland, Andrew.
    Modern American farm tractors/ Andrew Morland.
      p.   cm. -- (Enthusiast color series)
    Includes index.
    ISBN 0-87938-926-5
    1. Farm tractors--United States--History. I. Title. II. Series.
    TL233.M568 1994
    629.225--dc20

                  94-5339
                  CIP

On the front Cover: This 1991 Ford Versatile 976 articulated four-wheel drive tractor uses the six cylinder Cummins turbocharged diesel engine of 855ci. In 1989 Ford bought the Versatile Farm Equipment Company of Winnipeg, Manitoba, where the Ford Versatile line of supertractors are still built. Owner, Brian Brekken of Dennison, MN.

On the back cover: This Steiger 1360 "Panther" belongs to farmer Paul Frank of Redwood Falls, Minnesota. The articulated 4WD tractor is powered by the six cylinder 893ci Caterpillar engine. The transmission has twenty forward speeds and four reverse speeds.

On the frontispiece: The Versatile 256 uses the four cylinder turbocharged 239ci Cummins diesel engine, producing 84 horsepower. The Versatile 276 used the same 239ci Cummins engine, but with an intercooler.

On the title page: These two Fords are collecting grass for silage. The tractor in the foreground is a Ford 8210 built in 1989, with a six cylinder turbocharged diesel engine producing 120 hp. The manual transmission has sixteen forward and four reverse gears. The other tractor is a 1987, TW15 Series II six cylinder turbocharged diesel of 130hp. Its transmission is a manual sixteen forward speed and four reverse. The owners, who farm in Somerset, England claim to have 11,000 hours on this tractor.

Printed and bound in Hong Kong

Contents

Acknowledgments   6

Introduction   7

Chapter 1   Massey-Ferguson   9

Chapter 2   Case International   19

Chapter 3   White & Allis-Chalmers   33

Chapter 4   Oliver, Big Bud, Minneapolis-Moline & Terra-Gator   49

Chapter 5   Steiger, Versatile & Caterpillar   65

Chapter 6   Ford & John Deere *by Robert N. Pripps*   77

Index   96

Acknowledgments

Thank you to all the farmers and tractor enthusiasts for allowing me to photograph their tractors. Their cooperation has made this book possible.

A special thank you goes to Allen Higley and Leslie Stegh of John Deere and Company. Also thanks to John Briscoe of the Massey-Ferguson Group for crucial information, historic photographs, and cut aways.

Further thanks to the Case International dealer Harms Implement Co. of Everly, Iowa, and the AGCO, Massey-Ferguson, Ford, New Holland dealer Weltsch Equipment, Inc., of Redwood Falls, Minnesota.

Introduction

The development of the farm tractor from the 1960s to the 1990s has seen many changes. No single company is responsible. In 1963 John Deere launched the six-cylinder 4020 tractor which influenced tractor design for many years. Massey-Ferguson's DX development project of 1965, with its new range of M-F tractors, was equally successful. The turbochargers first used on the Allis-Chalmers D19 diesel tractor were refined by the Garrett Corporation for the powerful tractors of today. Goodyear developed the "Terra-Tire" flotation tire, which has a wider cross-section and more flexible carcass, and therefore gives a large load area with low ground pressure for farmers with a soil compaction problem. Four-wheel drive and hydraulic power assisted front-wheel drive have become more common and necessary as the size and power of tractors have increased. Automated controls and information systems with computers and radar have made tractors more efficient and farmers more productive.

Tractor sales up to 1973 were booming, but the Arab-Israeli War of 1973-74 changed things drastically. OPEC reduced the production of oil until Israeli forces withdrew from the occupied territories and fuel prices increased dramatically. The result of this price increase was a massive collapse in sales for the tractor companies. The tractor companies had invested heavily in the construction industry, but the home market found that costs had escalated and work was stopped. The Third World market collapsed and the countries without oil could no longer afford big construction projects.

By 1980 tractor sales in the western world were approximately 808,000. In 1985 the figure had shrunk to 683,000. In 1992, the total figure was down to 536,000, due to the recession and uncertainty in farmers' incomes in America and in Europe.

However, John Deere still has the best selling tractors in America. Massey-Ferguson still has the best selling tractors in the world, not including the former Soviet Union and Eastern Bloc countries.

Chapter 1

Massey-Ferguson

The Massey-Ferguson story is one of cooperation. M-F is the product of deals, handshakes, and mergers, with the pivotal bespectacled figure of Harry Ferguson providing the driving force.

Far from being a lone inventor, Harry Ferguson was a practical man who realized that he needed partners to help build his creations. Born in 1884 in Northern Ireland, he came from a family of eleven, a farmer's son with a strong talent and interest in machinery. Early days spent selling tractors taught him the drawbacks of those primitive machines. They were cumbersome and dangerous, and manhandling attachments was heavy, awkward work. Harry's solution was three-fold. His prototype tractor, in resplendent gloss black, was a lightweight 1,792lb. It had a hydraulic lift system built in for easy use of the implement, and the three-

Left
Massey-Ferguson 3630
Built between 1987 and 1990, the 3630 used the six cylinder Perkins 365ci diesel engine of 133hp.

point mounting system improved both traction and safety. First it was built by David Brown of Huddersfield, then a handshake with Henry Ford made the Ford-Ferguson tractor a mass production reality. When the Ford agreement turned sour, Ferguson enlisted Sir John Black of the Standard company to build his tractors.

Toronto-based Massey-Harris sold other people's tractors at first: the Bull, the Parret and the Wallis Cub. Not until 1938 was there a genuine Massey-Harris, born and bred.

Massey-Harris had been upset by the success of the Ford-Ferguson and so was receptive when Harry offered to sell his entire tractor business. In 1953 Massey-Harris-Ferguson was born, soon to lose the Harris bit. At first, it looked as though the two companies would keep on ploughing separate furrows (for want of a better phrase) but from the mid-fifties on, the inevitable rationalization made itself felt.

By 1965, the process was complete. There were numerous factories: Detroit,

Massey-Ferguson 3095
A 3095 with six cylinder Perkins diesel engine of 365ci with a New Holland Round Baler in tow. The excellent "Dynashift" powershift transmission gives electronically controlled smooth power changes to the thirtytwo speed forward transmission. In the background a New Holland Combine Harvester is threshing wheat.

Toronto, Coventry, Beauvais, Fabbrico. All were contributing to a broad range of tractors, sold through a unified spread of M-F dealers across the western world. But if anything, that range was starting to look a little old fashioned, and the DX tractors announced in 1965 brought a new competitiveness. From the little MF135 to the Caterpillar-powered 1805, the DX really marked a turning point in the M-F range. Its real strength, though, was that Massey specialized in farming implements, whereas Ferguson had developed tremendous tractor expertise. This permitted the growth of a very strong, unified range of products that achieved a significant share of the world market. That success in turn financed the acquisition of other smaller companies: Perkins in England, which secured a supply of proven diesel engines, and Landini, which helped them to gain entry to the Italian tractor market.

Since then, M-F's position as one of the major players has been beyond doubt, despite difficult times. It wasn't all smooth sailing though. The Detroit factory closed in 1983, and financial problems continued into the mid-eighties. Producing a broad range of tractors has helped, and also reflected growing affluence.

The 135 was a small, simple tractor, just right for small farmers. It deserves recognition not just because of its success, but because it was the spiritual successor to the popular T20, the "Little Grey Fergie."

Since the 135's *raison d'etre* was as a price leader, it naturally had a substantial list of options. The standard gearbox gave six forward speeds and two reverse, but eight- and twelve-speeders were also available. If that wasn't enough, you could have power steering, a gasoline engine (though by now most users saw the advantage of diesel), differential lock, independent pto, different seats . . . even the fenders could be dished or flat-topped! Rather more relevant to most users, it also had the Ferguson hydraulics which a whole generation of farmers had found to be invaluable. With a response control to check the rate of implement drop, it had a lift force of 3,158lb.

That was the 135, the best selling M-F since the old T20 Ferguson, and it survived right up to the mid-1970s. An interesting note: in 1957, three 135s became the first vehicles to reach the South Pole.

Traditional tractors were all very well, but there was also a growing market for something much more serious. There had been half-hearted attempts at four-wheel-drive tractors before, but nothing had really taken off. In the early 1970s, as implements became bigger and heavier, it was realized that simply slotting in a more powerful engine wasn't enough, especially with the age-old formula of two big rear wheels driving, and two small front wheels steering. What was needed was permanent four-wheel drive, with all wheels the same size to equalize traction.

M-F's response, which brought a lot of success, were the 1505 and 1805. These were just the start of a line of top-range M-F tractors. Both were built in America, with American engines: massive V-8 Caterpillar diesels. Turbochargers, rather than extra cubic inches, had become the preferred method of boost. Typical were the more recent 4840 and 4880. Since the Detroit factory closed, these supertractors have been built in Toronto. But M-F's biggest available models are still made in America, albeit by McConnel.

Electronics were not new to M-F when the 3000 series appeared in 1986, but they were now seeping down to mid-range

Massey-Ferguson 2775
The 2775 is powered by a Perkins V8 640 direct injection diesel. The 640ci engine has a bore of 4.63in and a stroke of 4.75in and is rated at 160pto hp at 2600rpm. A turbocharged version, the 2805, is rated at 190pto hp at 2500rpm.

machines for the first time. Basically, electronics replaced all the rods, levers and cables that had controlled the Ferguson hydraulic system for years. Not only was it simpler, but the new system allowed more accurate control. However, not everyone welcomed the electronic age. Rods and cables may need more adjustment, but they're easier to fix in the farmyard.

The 3000 range was big, and currently spans from an 80hp four-cylinder diesel to a six-cylinder turbo of 190hp, all of them being direct injection Perkins diesels. All but the most expensive were available with

Massey-Ferguson 180
Built in 1970, the 180 was powered by the four cylinder Perkins diesel engine of 236ci and produced 57pto hp. A gasoline version of the same capacity produced the same horsepower.

either two- or four-wheel drive.

By contrast the new Coventry-built 300 was altogether simpler: no electronics or 32-speed transmissions. It does the same basic job as the old 135, and even the T20 before that and because of this, is more suited to Third World markets. But even so, the 300 reflects the ever-growing demand for greater comfort and sophistication. The cab can feature a radio-cassette, extra soundproofing, even air conditioning—things have evidently changed since the T20. If it rained in those days, you got wet!

The M-F range has extended ever onwards and upwards, with more power, more features, more sophistication. By

Massey-Ferguson 135
Powered by the three cylinder Perkins diesel, the 135 was immensely successful world wide. The model shown here was built at the Beauvais Massey-Ferguson Factory in France and the photograph was taken in Normandy. The farmer is selling garlic from his trailer.

Massey-Ferguson 1250
The articulated four wheel drive tractor sold well in
North America and Europe. The 345ci six cylinder
Perkins diesel engine produced 112hp at
2500rpm with pto hp of 96. The transmission has
twelve forward speeds and four reverse speeds.

Massey-Ferguson 185
The 185 was built between 1971 and 1976 with the four cylinder Perkins diesel engine, producing 71pto hp.

Right
Massey-Ferguson 3115
This four-wheel drive high-tech tractor for the 1990's comes with "Autotronic," the automatic control of differential lock, gearbox power and to front axle power. Electronic linkage control for depth joined to a "Datatronic" onboard computer, providing information on twentytwo tractor functions including time, economy and types of implements used. The 3115 uses a six cylinder 365ci engine of 115 hp.

Above

Massey-Ferguson 398

This 1991 398 has a Perkins AT4 four cylinder turbocharged diesel engine of 236ci which produces 86pto hp. Four-wheel drive can be engaged on the go and there is a choice of a twelve forward speed manual shift, a single lever continuous eight or a twelve forward speed shuttle transmission.

Chapter 2

Case International

By 1985, the Tenneco organization could boast of three tractor companies in its make-up, two American and one British. J. I. Case & Co. joined Tenneco in the early seventies, along with David Brown Tractors, the English gear company which had built the Ferguson A in the 1930s. In 1984, with a high dollar and falling exports, International Harvester was forced to follow its old competitor into the arms of Tenneco. The names Case and International now appear side by side on a huge range of modern machinery.

Case entered the tractor market proper in 1910 as the J. I. Case Threshing Company. It built only cross-engine machines at

Left

Case International 1494 Hydra-Shift
The 1494 Hydra-Shift on its way to the farm, with a full load of grass for silage, driven by owner Doug Adams. The four cylinder 3594 cc diesel engine was built in 1988 and produces 78pto hp. The Hydra-Shift semi automatic transmission gives a choice of four speeds in creep, field, road and reverse, which translates to a twelve forward speed transmission.

first but in 1929 bowed to the inevitable with its unit-construction Model L.

The International Harvester Company was the result of a 1902 merger between McCormick and Deering. As the company grew, so did production: 78,000 of the model 10-20 Titans were built between 1915 and 1922. Of the 15-30, which followed, 160,000 were sold. Like Case, International began painting its tractors bright red in the 1930s (Case had found that changing from grey to red had actually helped sales); streamlined styling followed, and the range was massive.

The sixties and seventies saw some very clear trends in tractor design. There was the inexorable move toward diesel; by the late sixties, virtually everything tested at the famous Nebraska Tractor tests was diesel. Then there was the push for more power, more features, more comfort. The Case-Internationals that emerged in the late eighties reflected all of this, but the market for small basic machines wasn't abandoned altogether.

A 45hp two-wheel drive Case-IH with no

Case 1370
A 1370 Agri-King built in 1973 with six cylinder
Case turbocharged diesel of 504ci producing
140hp. The Case 12 forward speed power shift
transmission gave a top speed of 17.8mph.

Case 2470
The 2470 Traction King four wheel drive had a Case power shift transmission and four wheel steering. Built in 1972 with the Case six cylinder 504ci turbocharged diesel engine.

electronics or air conditioning was still available: the 395. This was the simplest and cheapest of the 95 series. This series ranged from the 395 up to the 90hp turbocharged 995 and helped to take Case-IH into the 1990s. It's interesting to compare these two, partly because they are representative of the company's small to mid-range machines, and partly because they show just how much variety can be built into one basic range.

At the other end of the scale there's the Magnum. First appearing in 1988, this was the first new tractor to emerge from Case-IH's joint development center. This new

Case 2590
The two wheel drive diesel tractor built in the early 1980s before International joined Tenneco.

Case International 956XL
Owner Alfred Chinnock in his 1988 956XL, and Forage Harvester behind, silage harvesting in Somerset, England. The XL stood for Luxury and Comfort Cab, with option of air conditioning not available on the L-Cab model.

series was officially known as the 7100 series, and like the 95s, all the engines were built in-house. The 7100 was actually a range of four tractors spanning 155–246hp, all of them four-wheel drive, turbocharged 8.3ltr direct injection six-cylinder diesels; only the power differentiated them. An optimistic Case-IH described it as "the most advanced diesel-powered engine available today." A sweeping statement but one that befitted a nineties top range tractor.

Case International 9280

Operator Chuck Robinson is dwarfed by the massive 9280. Built in 1991, the Steiger-built 12 wheeled tractor weighs in at 34,499lb. Steiger provides Case International's top of the line tractors with the six cylinder turbocharged intercooled Cummins NTA-855 diesel engine. The 855ci engine produces 375hp and gives a maximum torque of 1266lb-ft at only 1400rpm. This supertractor has a wheelbase of 141.5 inches and overall length of 279.5 inches. Height to top of exhaust just above the cab roof is 149.6 inches.

Case International 956XL and 1494

The 956XL and Forage Harvester on the left, cutting grass for silage. On the right, a Case International 1494 Hydra-Shift waits to swap the grass trailer.

Case International 9280
 The extra quiet cab with 51 square feet of tinted glass insulates the driver from the massive six cylinder Cummins diesel engine. "Comfort Master" air ride seat and air conditioning complete the luxury.

Case International 9280
Four-wheel drive is standard on the articulated frame 9280. It has a transmission with twelve forward speeds and three reverse with a continuous pulse shifter, plus a Skip-Shift control, with first to fourth to sixth to eighth gears for highway use. It also features the "Swinging Power Divider" drive line.

Case International 7140 Magnum
 The 7140 is powered by a six cylinder turbocharged, intercooled 505ci diesel engine producing 195pto hp. It has an eighteen speed Powershift transmission with continuous straight lever sequential changes. Lynda Zillmer is at the controls in the luxury "Silent Guardian II" cab in northern Wisconsin.

International 1066 Farmall
Built between 1971 and 1976, the six cylinder
International Harvester turbocharged engine of
414ci produced 108 to 125hp at 2600rpm. This
powerful tractor has sixteen forward gears.

Above
International 784
The 784 was built in Doncaster, Great Britain, with a German International D246 four cylinder diesel engine producing 80hp at 2,400rpm. the standard gearbox has eight forward gears and four reverse with double the number when the optional Torque Amplifier is fitted. It was said to have a maximum torque of 194.2lb-ft at 1600rpm. Its power steering uses piped hydraulics.

Left
International 966 Farmall
Built between 1971 and 1976, the 966 featured the "Year-A-Round" heavily upholstered cab, with a built in roll cage. The sixteen forward gears on this tractor give speeds of 1.5mph to 20.5mph. Its six cylinder, 414ci International Harvester engine produces 86 to 100hp. A "Hydro" 966 was offered with less power, 70 to 90hp, but with infinitely variable speeds up to 18mph.

Chapter 3

White & Allis-Chalmers

The White Motor Corporation of Cleveland, Ohio, one of the leading manufacturers of heavy trucks, bought the Oliver Corporation in November 1960. The new company's agricultural division was later named the White Farm Equipment Company. Tractors were produced at its Charles City, Iowa, plant. White purchased the Oliver-owned Cleveland Crawler Tractor Company (Cletrac) in 1962 and moved the crawler manufacturer to the Charles City plant, where it continued until 1965 when production ceased. White also bought the Canadian Cockshutt Farm Equipment Company in 1962, and then the Minneapolis-Moline Company in 1963. This amalgamation of the three big companies' production, range of models, and dealer network put the White Farm Equipment Company in an exceptional position in the tractor market.

White 4-150 Field Boss
Built from 1974 up to 1978, this articulated four-wheel drive tractor with Caterpillar power was the first tractor to be solely marketed as a "White."

Initially Cockshutt, Oliver and Minneapolis-Moline kept their own names, colors, and logos on the tractors, but in 1969 the White name was given equal importance. In 1971 the big articulated A4T Series 4WD was offered in full White livery, and in 1974 the new series of White "Field Boss" tractors took on the White colors, gray and silver, with no acknowledgment to the past heritage of the company.

From 1980 the owners of the White Farm Equipment Company changed regularly. In December 1980 Texas Investment Corporation bought the complete White Farm Equipment Company. In November 1985 Allied Products Corporation bought a large part of the White Farm Equipment Company and moved the headquarters to South Bend, Indiana.

In May 1987 the White Farm Equipment Company merged with the New Idea Farm Equipment Company and acquired a new name: the White-New Idea Farm Equipment Company.

In 1991 AGCO, headquartered in Nor-

White 4-150 Field Boss
The 4-150 Field Boss was powered by a V8
Caterpillar diesel engine of 636ci which produced
151hp at 2,800rpm.

White Plainsman
This model was built in late 1971. Known as the A4T series by White, this tractor was also marketed in Oliver, Minneapolis-Moline and Heritage colours. Owner Roger Mohr at the controls.

cross, Georgia, purchased the White tractor range. Today the successful White 6000 series is sold through AGCO Allis dealers, who also sell Deutz-Allis, Agco Allis and Massey-Ferguson tractors.

Allis-Chalmers

The Allis-Chalmers Company was formed in 1901 by the merger of four large companies: the Edward P. Allis Company of Milwaukee, Wisconsin; the Fraser and Chalmers Company of Chicago, Illinois; the

White Plainsman
The model shown here is the lp gas engine tractor A4T-1600 which produces 169 hp from the 504ci engine.

Right
White 2-60 Field Boss
A 2-60 Field Boss towing a New Holland baler and bales. The four cylinder 210.8ci was diesel built from 1976 to 1980 by Fiat in Italy.

Dickson Manufacturing Company of Pennsylvania; and the Gates Iron Works of Chicago. The first Allis-Chalmers tractor was the 15-13 built in 1918. In the early days, however, the most successful tractors were bought in from other companies.

In 1928 Allis-Chalmers bought the Monarch Tractor Incorporated company of Springfield, Illinois, and produced excellent

White American 60
Built in 1989 by the White-New Idea Farm
Equipment Company of Coldwater, Ohio, the 60
hp diesel engine tractor was the smallest
horsepower tractor built in North America in the
1980's.

White American 80
The model 80 was built in 1991 at the White-New Idea factory with a 239ci four cylinder diesel engine from Cummins. This model is painted in Minneapolis-Moline gold but it was also available in White silver gray, Oliver green and Cockshutt red.

Field Boss 2-70
The 2-70 was built from 1976 up to 1982. Shown
here is the six cylinder 265ci gasoline engine
which produces 70pto hp. The diesel six cylinder
also produces 70pto hp but from a 238ci engine.

Allis-Chalmers D-21
This Allis-Chalmers tractor had a six cylinder 426ci diesel engine and was built from 1963-1969. Offered with naturally aspirated 3400AC diesel engine or turbocharged 3500 AC diesel engine. Owned by Edwin and Larry Karg of Hutchinson, Minnesota.

A-C crawler tractors up until 1974, when the company merged with Fiat. In 1929, the consortium with the United Tractor and Implement Corporation of Chicago, produced the best selling Model "U." The Allis-Chalmers Company prospered during the period from the Second World War up to the 1960s.

Production of the famous D-19, the first production diesel to be fitted with a turbocharger, finished in 1964, but by 1965 the A-C's "D" range of tractors were becoming dated. In 1971 the Allis-Chalmers Company name was changed to Allis-Chalmers Corporation. The demand for tractors declined in the early 1980s and with production problems at Allis-Chalmers the company was sold to the Klockner-Humboldt-Deutz company of Germany, renamed the Deutz-Allis Corporation.

The last Allis-Chalmers tractor was built on 6 December 1985.

The Allis-Chalmers 4W305
The four wheel drive articulated Allis-Chalmers diesel engine tractor produced after the AC440 Steiger V8 Cummings engine ceased production in the 1970's. This 1983 model is owned by the Hoff family of Hutchinson, MN.

Allis-Chalmers "One Seventy"
This Allis-Chalmers is the gasoline 226ci four
cylinder engine model, producing 50hp. The "One
Seventy" was also available with 235.9ci four
cylinder diesel Perkins engine. Production was
from 1967 to 1973.

Above
Allis-Chalmers "One Ninety" XT Series III
The One Ninety XT diesel was in production from 1965 to 1972. The 301ci six cylinder Allis-Chalmers diesel was available in turbocharged 93hp or naturally aspirated 77hp versions. The 265ci gasoline engine produced 75hp and the 301ci LPG version 85 It had an eight forward speed transmission, giving a top speed of 13.6mph.

Right
Allis-Chalmers "One Ninety" XT Series III
The One-Ninety weighed 7,945 lbs and used an eight forward speed transmission, giving it a top speed of 13.6mph. This 1971 model is owned by Larry Karg of Hutchinson, Minnesota.

Duetz-Allis 9130
Built in 1991, the 9130 had two wheel drive and
four rear wheels. The German-built, Deutz air-
cooled diesel is economical in operation.

*The familiar A-C diamond trademark [was used by] the company from
its 1901 beginnings. The diamond underwent substantial changes and
modifications, but it nevertheless remained on all Allis-Chalmers
products from the smallest tractor to the largest steam turbine.*

—C.H. Wendel
Allis-Chalmers Tractors

Deutz-Allis 9130

The power front axle assistance model built in 1992, with air cooled Deutz diesel engine. The air cooled engine has quick warm up time and low maintenance costs with no radiators, water pumps and hoses.

Deutz-Allis 9130 (PFA)

The Hoff family on their Cedar View Farms at Hutchinson, Minnesota with one of their 9130s. Left to right Raymond, Gary and Jon.

Chapter 4

Oliver, Big Bud, Minneapolis-Moline & Terra-Gator

The Oliver Farm Equipment Company was formed in April 1929 by the merger of four large companies: the Oliver Chilled Plow Company of South Bend, Indiana; Nichols and Shepard Threshing Machine Company of Battle Creek, Michigan; American Seeding Machine Company of Springfield, Ohio; and the Hart-Parr Tractor Company of Madison, Wisconsin. James Oliver, a Scottish immigrant, started his company in 1855, and his son Joseph became chairman of the new company.

The Hart-Parr tractor company, formed by Charles Hart and Charles Parr, had produced the world's first successful internal combustion engined farm tractor. Hart-Parr is also acknowledged for creating the word "tractor." In 1930, Hart-Parr tractors were renamed Oliver Hart-Parr. Over the next few years the Oliver name became more and more dominant, until 1937, when Hart-Parr was dropped completely.

In November 1960 the Oliver Corporation was bought by the White Motor Corporation of Cleveland, Ohio, the largest builder of heavy trucks in the world. In 1962 White bought out the Oliver subsidiary Cockshutt Farm Equipment Company, which built combines. However, due to a depressed combine market this factory was closed in 1986.

In the mid-1970s the marketing department at the White Farm Equipment Company succeeded in killing off the Oliver name, and from then on produced tractors bearing only the White name. The 2255 built from 1973 up to 1976 is much sought after by Oliver Collectors, and is thought by many to be the last real Oliver tractor.

Left
Oliver 1855
Another Garnhart family tractor, this time a 1972 model 1855. The roll over protection is a period replica built by the Garnharts. The White Oliver six cylinder 310ci engine produced 98hp in diesel and 92hp in gasoline. An unusual item on this tractor is the gas tank in each fender, which gives an extra 39 gallons per side plus the regular tank. The 1855 was in production from 1969 to 1975.

Oliver 1655

This 1974 model 1655, with its 1610 sub loader frame, is owned and used on the farm by Rick and Andrew Garnhart in German Valley, Illinois. Production of the 1655 was from 1969 up to 1975. The diesel and gasoline engines were rated at 70hp with lp gas giving 66hp.

Oliver 2255
This 1973 model 2255 is owned and still used for farming by Lee Miller of German Valley, Illinois.

The 2255 was manufactured in Charles City, Iowa between 1973 and 1976.

Left
Oliver 1955
Rick Garnhart stands next to his dual tired 1972 model 1955, which still gives economical and reliable service on his farm. The six cylinder diesel produces 108 hp from its turbocharged 310ci engine.

Above

Oliver 2255

The 2255 was originally built with the 573ci V8 Caterpillar diesel engine producing 145pto hp. Later in its production run the 2255 was fitted with Caterpillar's 636ci diesel engine of 636ci with 147pto hp.

Big Bud

In 1968 the Northern Manufacturing Company of Havre, Montana, produced its first tractor, the impressive Big Bud. The company knew there was a market for extra powerful tractors because Steiger four-wheel drive tractors had been selling well since the late 1950s.

Right

The Oliver 2255

The Oliver 2255 was also sold as the White 2255 tractor. Its "Over/Under Hydraul Shift" gave plus or minus 20 percent in speed to the standard six speed transmission.

Big Bud 525/50
Built in 1981 by the Northern Manufacturing
Company of Havre, Montana, the six cylinder

1150ci turbocharged, intercooled Cummins diesel
engine produces 525hp.

The enormous Big Buds were produced for the large prairie farms of Canada and the United States. The "Big Bud" tractor's most important feature was tremendous horsepower, and it had reliable axles and a transmission that could take the power. It also had a clever arrangement of the engine, transmission and front radiator. These were mounted on a steel skin frame which could be removed for major servicing.

In the early 1970s the Northern Manufacturing Company offered more horsepower than the Steiger and Versatile tractor companies. Production and demand declined in the late 1970s with increased competition from International, Massey-Ferguson, Versatile, Steiger, and the John Deere engined 8000 Series.

Today many Big Buds are still in use. Although production stopped in the 1980s new spares are easy to obtain for engines and transmissions from dealers in Montana.

Big Bud 525/50
This 525/50 is painted in the standard white colour
scheme. It is owned and used by farmer Richard
Dahlgren on his large farm in Western Minnesota
at Bird Island.

Minneapolis-Moline

In 1929 the Minneapolis-Moline Power
Implement Company was formed by the
merger of the Moline Plow Company, the
Minneapolis Threshing Machine Company,
and the Minneapolis Steel Machinery Company. The Minneapolis-Moline Company
was bought by the White Motor Corporation

Right
Big Bud 525/50
The 1981 525/50 had a thirteen forward speed
transmission, with partial range power shift.

Minneapolis-Moline G1050

This lp gas tractor was built in 1971 at the Minneapolis, Minnesota plant. The 104 inch wheelbase tractor has a three speed "Ampli-torc" drive giving speeds of 1.67mph to 19.26mph, with the standard five speed gearbox. This G1050 has already become a classic collectors' tractor and is in the Roger Mohr Collection in Vail, Iowa.

in 1963.

The Minneapolis-Moline tractor slowly lost its identity in the 1960s. First the radiator was painted white, then a white stripe on the yellow and brown radiator surround gave an indication of the new owner. "Min-

neapolis-Moline," finally disappeared from tractors in favor of "White" in 1974, despite using M-M engines and being built in Minnesota. Two models built between 1973 and 1974 were the last Minneapolis-Moline tractors to carry the name.

Minneapolis-Moline G1050
The G1050's 504ci six cylinder engine
produced 110pto hp at 1800rpm. It was built from
1969 to 1971.

Minneapolis-Moline G1050
A closeup of the G1050. In 1971, White also
marketed this tractor as the Oliver 2055.

Minneapolis-Moline M670

Featured here is a 1969 gasoline version of the M670, with the four cylinder 336ci Minneapolis-Moline engine. This engine produces 73hp at 1600rpm. The lp gas engine of the same capacity produced 74hp at 1600rpm. This restored M670 is in the Roger Mohr collection.

Minneapolis-Moline opted for a continuation of the slower speed and longer stroke engines as being the best approach to maximum lugging power and longer engine life.

—C.H. Wendel
Minneapolis-Moline Tractors 1870-1969

Minneapolis-Moline G706
This tractor is an lp gas G706, built from 1962 to 1965. The G706 had four-wheel drive, while the G705 was the two-wheel drive version. The six cylinder Minneapolis-Moline 504ci engine produced 101hp at 1600rpm.

Right
Minneapolis-Moline M670
Built between 1964 and 1970, the M670 had a ten forward speed transmission, and could deliver speeds ranging from 1.6mph to 17.2mph.

Terra-Gator 1664T

This 1664T was built by AG-Chem Equipment Company, Inc. of Minnetonka, Minnesota in 1990. A specialist liquid sprayer and dry spreader, this tractor is powered by a Caterpillar 3208T turbo-charged V8 diesel producing 250 hp at 2800rpm. An automatic Allison MT-643 four forward speed transmission is standard, giving up to 24mph field speed and up to 30mph road speed.

Terra-Gator 1664T

The AG-Chem Terra-Gator is offered with manual ten speed Fuller Roadranger or automatic four speed Allison transmissions. It uses a quick change system from liquid sprayer to dry spreader systems. This gives the choice of 1550 U.S. gallon stainless tank for sprayer or dry system 234cu-ft open box.

Chapter 5

Steiger, Versatile & Caterpillar

Steiger

The Steiger Tractor Company was started by two brothers in their farm workshop in 1957. Douglas and Maurice Steiger built their first tractor for themselves. They needed a powerful four-wheel drive tractor for their farm in northwestern Minnesota, but none were offered by the major tractor companies. Most farmers were using powerful, expensive crawler tractors. At this time Harris in the United States and County in Great Britain built a good four-wheel drive, but they were not powerful enough.

Farming neighbors of the Steigers were impressed by their tractor and soon the orders were flowing in. The next few years saw the Steigers selling 120 tractors from the workshops on their farm. Sales were

Ford FW20

Marketed by Ford, but built by Steiger, this 1978 model is powered by the 555ci V8 Cummins diesel producing 210 horsepower. The transmission has 20 forward gears and four reverse gears.

mainly to the big wheat farmers of Alberta, Saskatchewan, Montana, and the Dakotas.

In 1963 Steiger produced their second series evolution models which would stay in production until 1969, when the Steiger Company moved production to Fargo, North Dakota. In 1972 Steiger built a 555ci V-8 Cummins diesel-engined four-wheel drive for Allis-Chalmers called the 440. It had Allis-Chalmers colors and styling, but the cab was pure Steiger.

Steiger was taken over by the International Case Tenneco organization in 1986.

Versatile

The Versatile Manufacturing Company of Winnipeg, Manitoba, in Canada, built their first four-wheel drive tractor in 1966. It was called the D100 and used the diesel six-cylinder Ford 363ci engine. An alternative cheaper gasoline model was also offered.

In 1967 a much improved and more powerful Versatile D-118 went into production. This model sold well to the big prairie farms of Manitoba and North Dakota. With

modifications, the D-118 stayed in production until 1971. In the mid-1970s the 800 Series Versatile articulated four-wheel drive went into production. This modern tractor immediately found sales over the whole of the prairie farmlands and later in the 1980s to a worldwide market.

However, from 1975 the big tractor market became very crowded. Massey-Ferguson, John Deere, Case, Steiger, International, and White were all offering four-wheel drive with lots of horsepower. The problem for Versatile was that the opposition tractors were often more sophisticated and the companies had bigger, more established dealer networks. This was especially so with Massey-Ferguson.

In 1989 Ford bought Versatile and production has continued of the articulated four-wheel drive Versatiles with improvements plus Ford badging and colors.

Caterpillar

In 1925 two companies, Best and Holt, merged to form the Caterpillar Company. Their model Twenty was built from 1927 to

Allis-Chalmers 440
The 440 was built by Steiger Tractor Inc. of Fargo, North Dakota, for Allis-Chalmers between 1972 and 1975. The 17,500 lbs four wheel drive articulated tractor is powered by the 555ci Cummins V8 diesel engine. Maximum power is rated at 208hp and the transmission has ten forward gears.

Steiger 1360
Paul Frank stands by his huge 1360 "Panther" in
which he has spent 2,800 hours working on his
farm in Minnesota.

Right
Steiger 1000
This closeup the 1000 "Puma" shows the
characteristic excellence of Steiger's cab design.
The forward and side visibility on the "Puma" is
better than in other Steigers which have the
muffler and air cleaner in view.

Versatile 256
This 1985 model 256 is a four-wheel drive loader tractor and has a very small turningcircle for working in confined spaces. The hydralastic three speed gearbox gives a top speed on the road of 18.5mph.

70

Versatile 256
Owner Larry Karg at the controls. Larry bought his 256 new and uses it mainly for snow blowing.

1933 and sold well despite the Depression. It was designed mainly for farm use and helped the Caterpillar Company grow in size and export worldwide.

Caterpillar's new tractor is the Challenger 65, designed specifically for farming. It is a tracked tractor as opposed to the conventional dual tire four-wheel drive tractor. It boasts twice the traction, half the compaction and has one-third of the ground pressure. This should provide much higher yield per acre for the farmer.

The "Mobil-trac System" uses a rubber

Versatile 555
The 555 is a four-wheel drive articulated tractor. Its manual transmission has fifteen forward speed gears but no power shift.

Versatile 555
Built in 1980, the 555 has a Cummins V8 diesel engine of 555ci producing 210hp. This tractor is owned and worked by Mat Feldman on his farm in Northfield, MN.

Caterpillar Challenger 65
Caterpillar's agricultural tractor. The six cylinder 638ci turbocharged and intercooled engine produced 285 hp at 2100rpm gross power. The pto power of 250hp at 1000rpm, and 225hp at the drawbar at 1900rpm can all be used with less ground slip, thanks to the "Mobil-trac" System and differential steering.

belt with four internal layers of flexible steel cables with outer rubber grooves for traction. The large contact area gives less than 6psi ground pressure. The front axle can move vertically and horizontally and the weight is evenly spaced by the mid-mounted bogie wheels.

Despite the many sales of large articulated four-wheel drive tire tractors over the past 20 years, sales of the new Challenger are increasing. There is also a demand for a smaller Challenger tractor, and Caterpillar is bound to have them in production before too long.

Caterpillar Challenger 65
This Challenger 65 is a 1990 model and is owned
by Stanton Phelps, who farms in Rockford, Illinois.

Chapter 6

Ford & John Deere

by Robert N. Pripps

Ford: 1965 to 1993
One: A Brief History

Henry Ford was raised on a prosperous farm in Michigan, near Detroit, but he detested the drudgery of farming. Even though his father gave him a forty of land when he turned twenty-one (in an effort to keep the young man on the farm), Henry logged it off, sold the lumber and went to Detroit. Nevertheless, as his mechanical abilities came to fruition, he never forgot the hapless farmer.

Henry Ford started the Ford Motor Company in 1903. To get it going, after several aborted attempts, Ford took in investors. As the business prospered, Ford chaffed under the control of these stockholders, feeling their restricting hand whenever he wanted to branch out in a new direction. This was

John Deere 4020
At the controls of this 1972 diesel 4020 (with cultivator attached) is Harold Schultz of Ollie, Iowa, who has put 6,000 hours on the six cylinder engine without any problems.

certainly true in 1914, when Henry determined to do for the farmer with a tractor what he had done for the motoring public with the Model T car.

To get away from stockholder interference, Ford formed a new and separate company to build his tractor; it was called Henry Ford and Son, Incorporated, and included his twenty-one year-old son, Edsel. By the time development testing was nearing completion, World War I was raging in Europe. To stave off massive food shortages in Britain, the British government placed an order for 6,000 of the new and yet nameless tractor in 1917. In the course of Transatlantic cable communications over the deal, the company name on the cablegrams was shortened to Fordson, and so the first Ford tractor got its name. Over 800,000 Fordsons were built by 1927. At that time, U.S. Fordson production was transferred first to Cork, Ireland, and later to Dagenham, England. Fordson production continued in several different models until 1964.

Meanwhile, in England, one Harry Fer-

Previous Page
Ford 5610
This 1990 model 5610 has a 256ci four cylinder diesel engine and is rated at 62 pto hp at 2100rpm. It has a standard eight speed transmission with the option of up to sixteen speeds "dual power."

Ford 6810
Farm contractor Ian Beer has worked 3750 hours in his 1990 four cylinder turbocharged 90 hp 6810. The manual "split gearbox" is easy to use and gives 32 gears. This tractor is fitted with the Ford radar option, which gives the useful warning of wheelslip: if wheelslip is over 15% it's time to stop work. The 6810 in the photo is pulling a Tanco round bale wrapper.

Ford 6600

This tractor, built in 1975 and still in everyday use, uses the four cylinder diesel engine of 255ci producing 70pto hp. The transmission is manual with eight forward gears and partial power range shift.

guson, and his team, invented the hydraulic three-point hitch with draft control. Unable to get his system into volume production in England, Ferguson turned to Henry Ford. The result was the famous Ford-Ferguson 9N, introduced in 1939. When Henry Ford II took over the company after the war, he soon recognized that Harry Ferguson was the only one making money with their relationship. He abrogated their agreement, and launched a revised tractor, the 8N in 1948.

Ferguson launched his own tractor company and a lawsuit against Ford for patent infringement. The suit forced Ford to redesign the hydraulic system, and therefore to upgrade the whole tractor. For the Golden Jubilee Fiftieth Anniversary of Ford Motor Company, Ford brought out the Model NAA in 1953. In 1961, Ford management launched a project to consolidate tractor models all over the world, and to eliminate competition between US and English tractors. Manufacturing centers were set up in Brazil, India, and several new locations in America and Great Britain. By 1965, the world tractor operation was in place.

Two: Modern Ford Tractors

The model 1000 was the proper successor to the 9N of 1939. This model was first introduced in 1973 especially for the part-time farmer. It was built for Ford by Ishikawajima Harima Industries of Japan.

Introduced in late 1971, the Model 7000 came later than the 8000 and 9000 in the grand scheme of things. Rated at 84hp, it was available in all-purpose and row-crop configurations. The 7000 was the first Ford tractor to use the Load Monitor, a sophisticated electro-hydraulic replacement for Harry Ferguson's draft control spring. It sensed drive line torque and adjusted implement depth accordingly. This feature was later incorporated into other Ford tractors as well.

The Model 8000 was introduced in early 1968 and was the first Ford to break the 100hp barrier. It was a big tractor in any league, using a 401ci six-cylinder diesel engine developing 105pto horsepower and weighing in at 11,000lb. It was also the first Ford tractor to be routinely offered with a fully enclosed cab.

Late in 1975, Ford Tractor Operations announced a completely new lineup for the 1976 model year: the 600 Series. The 700 Series would begin in 1977.

In late 1977, Ford entered into an agreement with Steiger Tractor, Inc., to market a line of four-wheel drive supertractors to be built by Steiger. This was the FW Series. Steiger was a pioneer in this field and also supplied such tractors to International Harvester as well as to their own dealers.

The TW Series of 1979 was an updated replacement for the 700 Series. Mechanical features remained the same, but styling for 1979 was added.

Three: The Modern Era

By 1980, the tractor line was maturing. All horsepower and weight classes were covered. Competitive positioning was now in the form of features, such as cabs, controls and instrumentation. The basic power trains did not change much from year to year.

Introduced for 1993, the Powerstar Series represents the absolute latest and finest in agricultural tractors. Comfort Command cabs and implement performance instrumentation are options, as is four-wheel drive. Transmission options include

Ford Versatile 976
In 1989 Ford bought the Versatile Farm Equipment Company of Winnipeg, Canada, where the Ford Versatile is built today. This 1991 976 is an articulated four-wheel drive with a six cylinder Cummins turbocharged diesel engine of 855ci. Owner, Brian Brekken of Dennison, MN.

the eight-speed manual, the eight-speed with partial range powershift, and two new shuttle transmissions that can be operated forwards or backwards in each of either six or eight gears.

In 1989, Ford bought the Versatile Farm Equipment Company of Winnipeg, Manitoba. It continued production of their line of articulated four-wheel drive tractors, with refinements and some model number changes. The model numbers included 846, 876, 946, 976, and the behemoth 1156 which used the Cummins six-cylinder turbocharged and intercooled diesel of 1150ci. This tractor, which had a working weight of 46,500lb, recorded a maximum drawbar pull of 43,219lb.

John Deere: 1965 to 1993
By the turn of the twentieth century,

Ford Versatile 976

The big diesel engine produces a small cloud of smoke at every gear change when using maximum rpm. This Versatile is the second biggest built in Winnipeg. The Versatile "1156" is the largest with its 1150ci six cylinder Cummins turbocharged and intercooled diesel engine.

John Deere 4020
The 4020 diesel built from 1964 to 1972, and was the most popular tractor of its decade in the U.S.

despite the farmers' unhappiness about the end of production of the popular two cylinder John Deere.

Deere & Company, the company founded in 1837 by blacksmith-plow maker John Deere was one of America's preeminent farm implement companies.

Also by the century's turn, a group of Waterloo, Iowa, businessmen had organized the Waterloo Gasoline Traction Engine Company around a successful sin-

gle-cylinder gasoline tractor built by John Froelich. The Waterloo company spawned the famed Waterloo Boy two-cylinder kerosene tractor in 1912.

In 1918, the directors of Deere decided that the highly regarded Waterloo Boy tractor, which was selling for $850, would be their ticket into the tractor market. Thus in

John Deere 4020
This cutaway showing some of the internal workings of the tractor. The six cylinder 404ci engine is a long stroke design for maximum torque. The bore is 4.25in and the stroke is 4.75in. It was available in diesel, gasoline or lp gas models.

Right
John Deere 4320
Built in 1970 with a six cylinder turbocharged 404ci diesel engine, this tractor produced 116.6pto hp at the Nebraska tests.

March of that year the Waterloo Gasoline Engine Company was purchased by Deere.

While Waterloo Boy production continued, Deere & Company proceeded with the development of improved farm tractors. Their goal was a tractor that could be operated by the average farmer at the lowest possible cost. After many experiments, it was decided to continue with the two-cylinder engine of the type used in the Waterloo Boy. This type of engine had fewer parts, simple rugged construction and low operating costs.

In 1924, the first two-cylinder tractor to bear the John Deere name was introduced. It was called the Model D. Its success was tremendous from the beginning, and, with a succession of updates, it stayed in production for the next thirty years.

The rugged Model D standard tread tractor could do some of the jobs around the farm, but it could not do them all. Farmers wanted a tractor that could replace the horse in jobs such as planting and cultivating. Therefore, in 1928, John Deere came out with the Model GP. It was the first tractor to incorporate a power-lift for its implements.

Following the Model GP, which, like the Model D, was a standard tread machine,

John Deere 4630
The 4630 was manufactured between 1973 and 1977 using a turbocharged 404ci diesel engine of six cylinders. It produced 135 drawbar hp and 150pto hp in the Nebraska tests.

came the row-crop Models A, B, G, and H with adjustable treads and hydraulic lifts. Different versions now proliferated, with standard tread and orchard versions of the row-crop machines. There also came crawler versions, smaller versions, larger versions, and versions with diesel engines. Eventually, as the mid-point of the twentieth century was passed, and tractor horsepowers exceeded seventy-five, the practicality of the two-cylinder engine came to an end.

At the end of the 1960 model year, John Deere came out with a completely new line of farm and industrial tractors. The development of this line had been underway for about seven years, and was one of the best-kept nonmilitary industrial secrets of all time. Brand new four- and six-cylinder vertical in-line engines powered the first four models and later a fifth model. The "New Generation" tractors, as they were called, had many features that were industry firsts.

In the late 1950s, Deere & Company began expanding production facilities to other countries. Facilities were established in Argentina and Mexico. In 1956, Deere acquired the German Lanz company. Later, facilities were added in France, Spain, South Africa and Australia. Finally, an arrangement was made with Yanmar Diesel Engine Company of Osaka, Japan, to manufacture tractors on the lower end of the power scale.

Between 1965 and 1972, there were sixteen models of John Deere tractors produced for America. (This is not counting the lawn and garden varieties begun in 1963). In most cases, the number designations for these sixteen models ended in 20, and are therefore known as the 20 Series. Then there was the Generation II tractors; the 30 Series; the 40 Series, known as the "Iron Horses;" the 50 Series; the 55 Series; the 60 Series and the current 6000-7000 Series with a plethora of variations on the model theme.

The turbocharger, long the darling of the race car driver and the aviator, had arrived to do its magic in the farm tractor. The turbocharger packed more air into the cylinders of an engine giving it an increase in power (a power increase equivalent to that of greater displacement), and at the same time, an efficiency increase which cut specific fuel consumption. The 4520 was the world's first turbocharged production tractor.

The articulated four-wheel drive tractor had been pioneered by Steiger and Wagner in the mid-1950s. In 1959, John Deere introduced their first version. Production ended in 1964. It wasn't until 1971 that another true John Deere articulated tractor, the Mod-

John Deere 3020
The 3020 was manufactured from 1964 up to 1972. The "Power Shift" transmission had eight forward and four reverse gears and hydraulic power takeoff for front and rear applications was standard. The three point hitch with Load-and-depth and rear power takeoff are clearly shown in the photograph.

John Deere 4250
Harold Schultz's 4250 with a liquid manure spreader on the farm in Ollie, Iowa. This 1983 model uses the six cylinder turbo diesel 466ci engine, producing 120pto hp.

John Deere 4430
Built from 1973 to 1977, the 4430 uses the turbocharged six cylinder 404ci diesel engine producing 125.9pto hp.

el 7020, was offered. In the meantime, two models of articulated tractors were made for John Deere by Wagner.

In 1987, engine improvements resulted in improved fuel economy. The 4000 Series of 1989 all had tremendous horsepower, and the 4955 was the first non-articulated John Deere to exceed 200hp. New was the electro-hydraulic version of Harry Ferguson's draft control system. The sixteen-speed Quad-Range transmission was standard on all but the 4955, which had the fif-

John Deere 7800

This top of the line 7000 Series tractor from 1992 uses the six cylinder turbocharged diesel of 466ci and produces 170 hp at 2100rpm. The three-point hitch is operated electro-hydraulically, and the "Power Quad" transmission offers twenty forward speeds.

teen-speed powershift. The powershift was available on the others as optional equipment.

By 1992, the 7000 Series offered the lat- est in power farming features. The 7800 used a six-cylinder turbocharged diesel of 466ci with 145hp. Mechanical front-wheel drive was optional and it had a maximum

John Deere 6400
These top of the line four cylinder diesels in the
6000 series produce 100hp from their 276ci
engine.

implement lift capacity of over 10,000lb.

The new ComfortGard cabs had all the
latest features and instrumentation. Even a
radar wheel slip indicator was available.

The PowrQuad transmission provided four
powershift speeds in each of four ranges. A
nineteen-speed powershift was optional.

Index

Allied Products Corporation, 33
Allis-Chalmers Company, 36, 41
Allis-Chalmers Corporation, 41
American Seeding Machine Company, 49
Black, Sir John, 9
Big Bud, 52
Caterpillar Company, 67
Cleveland Crawler Tractor Company (Cletrac), 33
Cockshutt Farm Equipment Company, 33
David Brown Tractors, 19
Deere & Company, 83
Deutz-Allis Corporation, 43
Ferguson, Harry, 9
Fiat, 41
Ford-Ferguson, 9
Ford, Henry, 9
Ford Motor Company, 77
Fordson, 77
Hart-Parr Tractor Company, 49
Henry Ford and Son, Incorporated, 77
International Harvester Company, 19
J.I. Case & Company, 19
J.I. Case Threshing Company, 19
Klockner-Humboldt-Deutz, 43
Massey-Ferguson, 9, 54, 67
Massey-Harris, 9
Minneapolis-Moline Company, 33
Minneapolis Steel Machinery Company, 55
Minneapolis Threshing Machine Company, 55
Minneapolis-Moline Power Implement Company, 55
Moline Plow Company, 55
Monarch Tractor Incorporated, 41
New Idea Farm Equipment Company, 35
Nichols and Shepard Threshing Machine Company, 49
Oliver Corporation, 33
Oliver Chilled Plow Company, 49
Oliver Farm Equipment Company, 49
Steiger Tractor Company, 65
Tenneco, 19
Texas Investment Corporation, 33
United Tractor and Implement Corporation, 41
Versatile Manufacturing Company, 65
Waterloo Gasoline Traction Engine Company, 85
White Farm Equipment Company, 33
White Motor Corporation, 33
White-New Idea Farm Equipment Company, 33

Tractor Models
Allis-Chalmers
    D-21, 41
    One Seventy, 43
    One Ninety XT, 44

4W305, 42
Big Bud
    525/50, 54, 55

Case
    1370, 20
    2470, 21
    2590, 22
Case International
    Magnum, 21
    395, 21
    956XL, 23, 25
    995, 21
    1494 Hydra-Shift, 19, 25
    7100 Series, 23
    7140 Magnum, 28
    9280, 24, 26, 27
Caterpillar
    Challenger 65, 71, 74, 75
Deutz-Allis
    9130, 46, 47
Ferguson
    T20 ("Little Grey Fergie"), 11, 13
Ford
    Powerstar Series, 82
    Steiger FW Series, 82
    TW Series, 82
    Versatile 846, 83
    Versatile 876, 83
    Versatile 946, 83
    Versatile 976, 83, 84
    Versatile 1156, 83
    600 Series, 82
    700 Series, 82
    5610, 80
    6600, 81
    6810, 80
    7000, 82
    8000, 82
    9000, 82
International
    784, 31
    966 Farmall, 31
    1066 Farmall, 29
John Deere
    Model D, 88
    Model GP, 88
    Waterloo Boy, 85
    20 Series, 90
    30 Series, 90
    40 Series, 90
    50 Series, 90
    55 Series, 90
    60 Series, 90
    3020, 90
    4000 Series, 93

4020, 77, 85, 86
4250, 92
4320, 86
4430, 93
4520, 90
4630, 88
4955, 93
6000 Series, 90
6400, 95
7000 Series, 90
7020, 93
7800, 94
Massey-Ferguson
    DX, 10
    180, 13
    135, 10, 13, 14
    185, 16
    398, 17
    1250, 15
    1505, 11
    1805, 10, 11
    2775, 12
    3095, 10
    3115, 16
    3630, 9
    4840, 11
    4880, 11
Minneapolis-Moline
    G1050, 56-58
    G706, 60
    M670, 59, 60
Oliver
    1655, 50
    1855, 49
    1955, 51
    2255, 49, 51, 52
Steiger
    Allis-Chalmers 440, 67
    Ford FW20, 65
    1000, 68
    1360, 68
Terra-Gator
    1664T, 62
Versatile
    D-100, 65
    D-118, 65
    256, 70, 71
    555, 73
    800 Series, 67
White
    American 60, 38
    American 80, 39
    A4T-1600 Plainsman, 35, 36
    2-60 Field Boss, 36
    2-70 Field Boss, 40
    4-150 Field Boss, 33, 34